Rhonda Hess

To Hannah, Mom, Uncle Homer, Aunt Glenna, Doug, Sally, David, Michael and Sarah.
L.W.

To my pals, Cory, Robin, Ian and Kshanika.
Karen

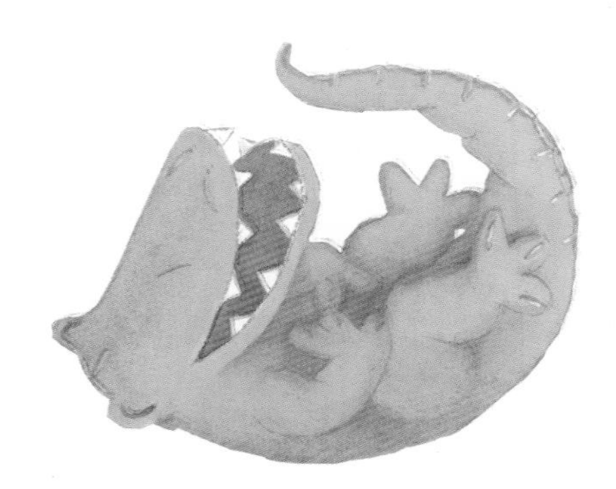

Broadman & Holman Publishers
127 Ninth Avenue, North, Nashville, TN 37234

Cover and interior design by Susan L. Chamberlain

Printed and bound in Italy.
SB134MLKJIHGFEDCBA
ISBN: 0-8054-1719-2

Mommy, Would God Still Love Me?

LAURA WALLACE
pictures by KAREN A. JEROME

Mommy, would God still love me
if I threw down all my clothes

and my bedroom was so messy
that I couldn't see my toes?

Mommy, would God still love me
if I lost my table manners

and thumped my spoon and banged my fork
like they were mighty hammers?

Mommy, would God still love me
if I drew outside the lines

and when my work was finally done
it looked like wiggly vines?

Mommy, would God still love me
if I saw a funny play

that made me laugh and shout so loud
that others moved away?

Mommy, would God still love me
if I pinched my little sister,

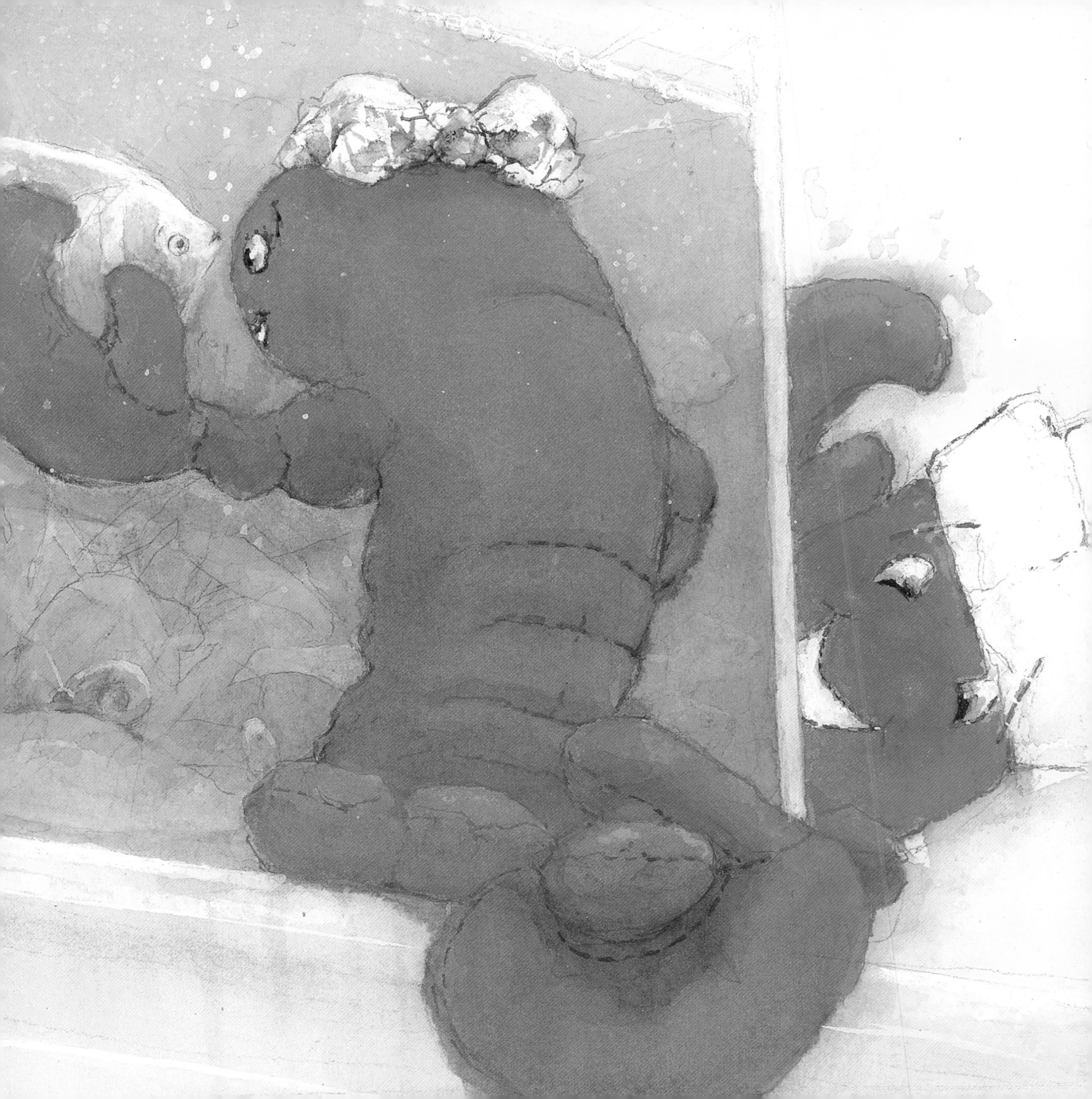

then said it was an accident,
I really meant to kiss her?

Oh yes, God loves us very much
Even when we do things wrong.
We cannot hide or run away,
His love is much too strong.

And when the things you do are kind
and the words you say are true,
it makes me glad, and I say a prayer,
"Thank you, God, for the wonderful
gift of You!"